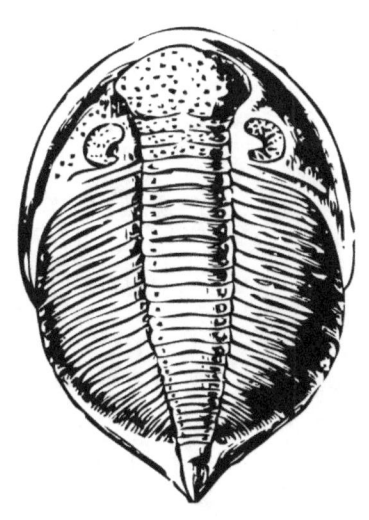

IN THE
BEGINNING

STEVEN R. MARTINS

IN THE
BEGINNING

STEVEN R. MARTINS

cántaro
publications

A PUBLISHING IMPRINT OF THE CÁNTARO INSTITUTE

cántaro
publications

cantaroinstitute.org

In the Beginning

Published by Cántaro Publications, a publishing imprint of the Cántaro Institute, Jordan Station, Ontario, Canada

For volume pricing, please contact
info@cantaroinstitute.org

Library & Archives Canada

ISBN: 978-1-990771-05-7

Printed in the United States of America

TABLE OF CONTENTS

"In the beginning, God created the heavens and the earth."

– Genesis 1:1

CHAPTER

1

THE QUESTION OF ORIGINS

EVERY WORLD-AND-LIFE VIEW, or philosophy of life, must answer four fundamental questions regarding reality: (i) What is the origin of all things? (ii) What is the meaning or purpose of the universe? (iii) What moral standards are we to live by? And (iv) What is the destined end of our created material universe? We might regard these questions, whether posed cosmologically or existentially, as four worldview aspects: origin, meaning, morality and destiny. However, no worldview can rightly respond to the latter three questions if a right and true answer is not first given to the question of origins, for this ultimately determines the intelligibility of a given worldview; either succeeding to make sense of our world in its interpretation, or rendering our perception logically inconsistent, and by implication, unintelligible.[1]

The Christian world-and-life view, like all other worldviews, is built upon its answer to the question

1. John D. Currid, "The Hebrew World-and-Life View" in *Revolutions in Worldview: Understanding the Flow of Western Thought*, eds. W. Andrew Hoffecker (Phillipsburg, NJ.: P&R Publishing, 2007), 49.

of origins. It is, in other words, its foundation. But unlike any other worldview, it is the only perception and interpretation of reality in which the predication of reality is made possible, that is, that as divine image bearers, we have the God-given capacity to make sense of creation. It can be said, in fact, that the Christian worldview is in a league of its own, being the only true worldview in which we can make perfect sense of our reality. The reason for this is rooted in the fact that the Christian world-and-life view provides a right and true answer to the question of origins, that is to say, an answer which adequately corresponds to reality, an answer which agrees with the witness of God's revelation, and an answer that is logically consistent and coherent with the whole Christian worldview. It provides, in other words, the necessary preconditions of intelligibility, what must be presupposed in order to make sense of, and to rightly live in, the world as we know it today. As the theologian James R. Mook rightly noted, "The opening chapters of Genesis are the most foundational in all of Scripture. Indeed... nothing makes lasting sense if these chapters are undermined."[2]

In the first three chapters of Genesis, we are provided with the biblical creation narrative, the first dealing with the creation of the cosmos, the second, a more focused creation of man, and the third, the fall of man and the corruption of creation – which, though it does not involve any creative activity, it does, nonetheless, provide us with the context to understand our present world. In recent years, scores of different interpretations have emerged for this biblical creation narrative, some variations classifying as progressive creationism, others as theistic evolution, and what has been more popular of late, the functionalism of ancient cosmology, according to the thesis of John H. Walton's *The Lost World of Genesis One*.

There have been several attempts to interpret Genesis from different, varying perspectives, more

2. James R. Mook, "The Church Fathers on Genesis, the Flood, and the Age of the Earth," *Coming to Grips with Genesis: Biblical Authority and the Age of the Earth*, eds. Terry Mortenson and Thane H. Ury (Green Forest, AR.: Master Books, 2012), 24.

attuned, some suggest, to the world's scientific understanding of natural history, but amid this plethora
of interpretations, the historic, literal creationist interpretation still persists. It is this interpretation, in
particular, which rightly reflects and affirms the being
and attributes of the God of Christian theism as por-
trayed in His special, written revelation. And, in fact,
it is the right and true interpretation according to the
witness of Scripture, as affirmed by conservative exegetes who uphold biblical authority, and as per the
testimony of the early church patristics. To deny this
interpretation is to undermine the biblical doctrine of
God and the Christian world-and-life view as a whole.
This is my objective, to demonstrate this fact. Ultimately, this denial implies altering God's character
and attributes to that which is foreign to Scripture, a
different and antithetical conception of God, which
renders, as a result, an entirely different worldview. To
adopt such a distortion of the truth results in severe
theological and epistemological complications, for to
adopt a non-biblical cosmology is to err in the same
way that the natural man errs, failing to make sense

of our reality because of the absence of the preconditions of intelligibility, or, in other words, what must
be presupposed in order to make sense of our reality,
that being the very same presuppositions of Scripture.

CHAPTER

2

A PROGRESSIVE
EARTH

PRESENTLY, ONE OF the most common and divisive interpretations of Genesis 1-3 is progressive creationism, otherwise known as the 'day-age' theory. This interpretation is largely built on supposed 'neutral' scientific findings, considering that, in spite of its claim of the sufficiency, inerrancy and infallibility of Scripture, there is a heavy reliance on the secular natural sciences for the building of a Christian cosmology. Not everything in the secular natural sciences are readily accepted, such as, for example, evolution as a means of God's creative process. But other theoretical components, not considered openly contradictory to the Scriptures, are imported into the cosmological composition of progressive creationism, like the timetable of the Big Bang cosmology, the "millions of years that separated the (miraculous) appearance of the various kinds of living things,"[3] or Charles Lyell's (1797-1875) theory of geological uniformitarianism, the theory that the earth is millions of years old based

3. John C. Whitcomb, "Progressive Creationism," in Institute for Creation Research, *Impact: Vital Articles on Science/Creation* (June, 2003), 1.

on the present rate of geological processes.

The interpretation method of progressive creationism in actuality reflects a pick-and-choose approach in terms of what theses might fit the Genesis creation narrative; what runs contrary to it, what should be discarded, and what might be "smuggled" in, all while ignoring the anti-biblical worldviews it imports from. In this interpretation's denial of the sufficiency of Scripture, that is to say, in not heeding God's written revelation as the ultimate authority for all knowledge, a foreign conception of theism is developed that stands in stark contrast and opposition to the Christian theism of the Bible. It is God's written revelation, after all, that provides us with the lens by which we can truly see and interpret the world, and that includes the sciences. But if that lens be removed or somehow fused with another, only a false, distorted interpretation of reality is possible, and that includes a distorted perception of God Himself.

A prominent Christian organization that advocates for progressive creationism is Reasons to Believe

(RTB), a scientific thinktank founded by astrophysicist Hugh Ross in 1986. Ross is considered one of the present leaders of the progressive creationist movement, having assembled a team of scholars and scientists for the advancement of progressive creationism. To articulate RTB's position on Christian cosmology, Ross states that our starting point must first be conceiving 'nature' as God's 67th book of Scripture, and by this he means that nature, like God's written revelation, serves as 'propositional revelation.'[4] However, in this statement, Ross already commits an epistemological error, because though nature may be one of the two aspects of God's unified revelation (special and general), it is not propositional. In fact, its data must first be interpreted according to a framework, a set of presuppositions concerning reality. Ross, in other words, believes that the facts and evidences of nature are 'brute' facts, that is to say, taken as a given and independent of God. This means that both the Chris-

---

4. Hugh Ross, *Creation and Time: A Biblical and Scientific Perspective on the Creation-Date Controversy* (Colorado Springs, CO.: NavPress, 1994), 56-57.

tian and the natural man can agree on these facts at some imaginary, neutral ground, all the while ignoring the fact that a person cannot help but interpret the evidence from a non-neutral position, that is to say, according to their own worldview.

RTB's conception of the facts then is that of brute, *uninterpreted* facts. However, geneticist and evolutionist Richard Lewontin disagrees with this notion of neutrality in factual interpretation:

> We take the side of science *in spite* of the patent absurdity of some of its constructs, in spite of its failure to fulfill many of its extravagant promises of health and life, in spite of the tolerance of the scientific community for unsubstantiated just-so stories, because we have a *prior commitment*, a commitment to materialism...[5]

Stephen Gordon, economist and professor at Université Laval, likewise notes that "Data cannot

5. Richard Lewontin, "Billions and Billions of Demons," *The New York Review* (January 9, 1997), 31. [emphasis added]

speak for themselves; they have to be interpreted through a theoretical model."[6]

The very notion of brute, uninterpreted facts contradicts the biblical understanding of facts and evidences as being *God's facts and evidences*, because ultimately, everything bears the mark of the Creator, everything is under His dominion. Facts and evidences, therefore, can only be properly interpreted when we think God's thoughts after Him, that is to say, when we adhere to God's Word as the ultimate authority for all knowledge. It is only then that we can comprehend God's general revelation in nature, for as the reformed theologian Louis Berkhof had put it:

> Since the entrance of sin into the world, man can gather true knowledge about God from His general revelation only if he studies it in the light of Scripture, in which the elements

---

6. Stephen Gordon, "Economists and their Data (so, so much data)," *National Post.* Accessed November 30, 2017, http://nationalpost.com/opinion/stephen-gordon-economists-and-their-data-so-so-much-data/.

> of God's original self-revelation, which were
> obscured and perverted by the blight of sin,
> are republished, corrected and interpreted.[7]

This implies that the natural man is helpless in the sense that, though he may study what is placed before him, that is, what constitutes as 'immediate knowledge,' he cannot make sense of that which he studies, because it is incongruent with his own presuppositions or worldview.[8] Ross commits the same error here in that he does not heed to Scripture as his epistemological authority, or in other words, that he does not heed to God's Word as his 'ultimate starting point' in his thinking,[9] and instead uses "long-age interpretations of nature to reinterpret the written

7. Louis Berkhof, Introductory Volume to *Systematic Theology* (Grand Rapids, MI.: Wm. B. Eerdmans Publishing Co., 1932), 60.

8. Cornelius Van Til, *A Survey of Christian Epistemology, Vol. 2 of the Series In Defense of Biblical Christianity* (Phillipsburg, NJ.: Presbyterian and Reformed Publishing Co., 1969), 106.

9. Ibid.

Word of God."[10]

Given progressive creationism's tendency to supplant Scripture with the findings and theories of secular science, it is not altogether surprising that in his hermeneutic, Ross makes an appeal to the broad semantic range of *yom* (day) to justify his unorthodox interpretation of Genesis 1-3. He essentially disguises his eisegesis for exegesis, as displayed for example in his book *The Genesis Question*:

> In English, the word *day* enjoys flexible usage. We refer to the day of the dinosaurs and the day of the Romans, and no one misunderstands our meaning. But we recognize this usage as figurative, acknowledging just two literal definitions: a twenty-four hour period, from midnight to midnight, and the daylight hours (roughly twelve, but varying

10. Jonathan Sarfati, *Refuting Compromise: A Biblical and Scientific Refutation of "Progressive Creationism" (Billions of Years) as Popularized by Astronomer Hugh Ross* (Green Forest, AR.: Master Books, 2004), 35.

from one latitude and season to another).[11]

Ross' argument is that *yom* should not be solely limited to its literal meaning but also expanded to its figurative expression, given that such flexibility is evident in its biblical usage. No Christian would argue against this flexible usage in Scripture, whether they identify as a progressivist, evolutionist, or creationist. However, as it relates to Genesis 1, Ross believes that the only acceptable interpretation of *yom* is non-literal, substituting 'day' in its literal sense for the figurative expression of 'ages.'[12] Only then can we reconcile natural science and Scripture, he reasons. But again, Ross commits an error, this time committing a grave exegetical fallacy, and scholar Jonathan Sarfati exposes this in his book *Refuting Compromise*, writing: "…the meaning of a word must be determined by how it is used in the specific context, not by possible meanings

---

11. Hugh Ross, *The Genesis Question: Scientific Advances and the Accuracy of Genesis* (Colorado Springs, CO.: NavPress, 1998), 65.

12. Ibid., 86.

(yom)

day

GENESIS 1:5

in unrelated contexts."[13] This fallacy is expounded by scholar D.A. Carson, who defines this example as an:

> Unwarranted expansion of an expanded semantic field. The fallacy in this instance lies in the supposition that the meaning of the word in a specific context is much broader than the context itself allows and may bring with it the word's entire semantic range.[14]

This same mistake is committed by those who insist on justifying their old-earth interpretation with the biblical passage of 2 Peter 3:8-9, which states:

---

13. Sarfati, *Refuting Compromise*, 69.

14. D.A. Carson, *Exegetical Fallacies*, 2nd Edition (Grand Rapids, MI.: Baker Book House, 1996), 60.; Carson could be said to be a theological ally of Ross in regard to origins, he unfortunately does not see this same error in his own interpretation. For more on this, see Simon Turpin, "Influential Pastors and Theologians on the Days of Creation and the Age of the Earth", *Answers in Genesis*. Accessed February 27, 2020, https://answersingenesis.org/creationism/old-earth/influential-pastors-and-theologians-on-the-days-of-creation-and-the-age-of-the-earth/.

> But do not overlook this one fact, beloved, that with the Lord *one day is as a thousand years, and a thousand years as one day.* The Lord is not slow to fulfill his promise as some count slowness, but is patient toward you, not wishing that any should perish, but that all should reach repentance.

We must first take into consideration that this passage has nothing to do with the Genesis creation narrative, it is unrelated. It cannot therefore be referred to as an *interpretation* of Genesis 1-3. Secondly, the word 'day,' in the Greek *hēmera*, is used in a different context here. In fact, as the text says, "one day is *like* a thousand years," the word "like" indicates that this is a figure of speech, a *simile* to teach God's transcendence, that he is not constrained to time and space because he is the Creator, and the Creator cannot be subject to His own creational law.[15]

The notion that somehow "long ages and therefore an old earth" is biblical is actually the result of

15. Sarfati, *Refuting Compromise*, 86.

eisegesis, not exegesis, considering that there is no textual evidence to suggest this. In fact, we would otherwise have to explain the awkward incongruence of Genesis 1-3 with the rest of Scripture, if the 'day-age' theory were adopted. As a result, it can be rightly said that progressive creationism is not the true interpretation of the Genesis creation narrative, but for those who claim that it is, they claim this in spite of the exegetical fallacies they commit and the gross theological distortion this causes to biblical theism. Consider, for example, how the origin of death and suffering, according to the progressive creationist, affects the doctrine of God and the Christian world-and-life view as a whole.

Progressive creationism argues that death and suffering were existent prior to the fall of Adam and Eve. This means that the fossil record – the millions of dead organisms buried in the rock layers – and the diseases found in fossilized specimens,[16] are not due

16. See for example "Dinosaurs suffered from Cancer too," *The Guardian*. Accessed December 12, 2017. https://www.theguardian.com/science/2003/oct/23/dinosaurs.science/.

to the fall in Genesis 3. This is the progressive creationist's framework, having adopted Lyell's geological
uniformitarian timeline of millions of years. And to
clarify what is meant by death and suffering: it is the
death and suffering of *nephesh chayyah*, Hebrew for
"living creatures," not plants and vegetation. This implies that God's proclamation of His creation as "very
good" (Gen. 1:31) includes death and suffering.[17] And
this is by no means a strawman portrayal of the day-
age theory, because the philosopher Holmes Rolston
II writes in agreement that the absence of death and
suffering prior to Adam and Eve is an impossibility
because it "does not fit into the biological paradigm at
all. Suffering in a harsh world did not enter chrono-
logically after sin and on account of it."[18] Ross joins
with him in denying the biblical teaching of the origin
of death and suffering, writing:

> While the sin we humans commit causes us

---

17. Sarfati, *Refuting Compromise*, 195.

18. Holmes Rolston, III. "Does Nature Need to be Re-
    deemed?" *Zygon*, vol. 29 (June 1994), 205.

all to react negatively to decay, work, physical death, pain and suffering... there is nothing in Scripture that compels us to conclude that none of these entities existed before Adam's first act of rebellion against God.[19]

But can we make sense of this? When a person created in God's image discovers that their body is giving way to cancer, can it be said "It is simply a part of God's good creation?" If a family dog is run over by a car, can it be said, "He experienced the goodness of death and suffering?" If nearby livestock were to be buried alive by a mudslide, could it be said that "They experienced a 'good event' in God's creation"? This notion of a "good" (*tov*) creation which includes death and suffering is reduced to an unintelligible absurdity, incongruent with the whole counsel of God's Word. The God of life is suddenly cast into the dark as the god of death, and the definition of goodness is now called into question as it is inseparably linked to the person of this different god; what a contrast that is

---

19. Ross, *Creation and Time*, 69.

to the true Christian world-and-life view.

It is no wonder then that Ross attempts to re-interpret the word "good" in Genesis 1, committing the same fallacy of an unwarranted expansion of an expanded semantic field, stating: "God's very good creation does not mean that it is 'perfect.' Most occurrences of this phase (*tov me'od*) are translated as 'very beautiful' or 'very wonderful.'"[20] However, God does not use the words "beautiful" or "wonderful," otherwise Bible translations would have used these terms. It is only by understanding God's true person according to the Scriptures, as wholly good, just and holy, and reconciling His person with the context of Genesis 1, that we can understand what God meant by "very good." It is contrary to the evil of death, disease and suffering which befell the created world in Genesis 3. It is the reflection of the moral attributes of God's very person. To posit that the biblical God created such a

20. Hugh Ross, Fazale Rana, Kenneth Samples, M. Harman and K. Bontranger, "Life and Death in Eden, The Biblical and Scientific Evidence for Animal Death Before the Fall," audio cassette set, Reasons to Believe, 2001.

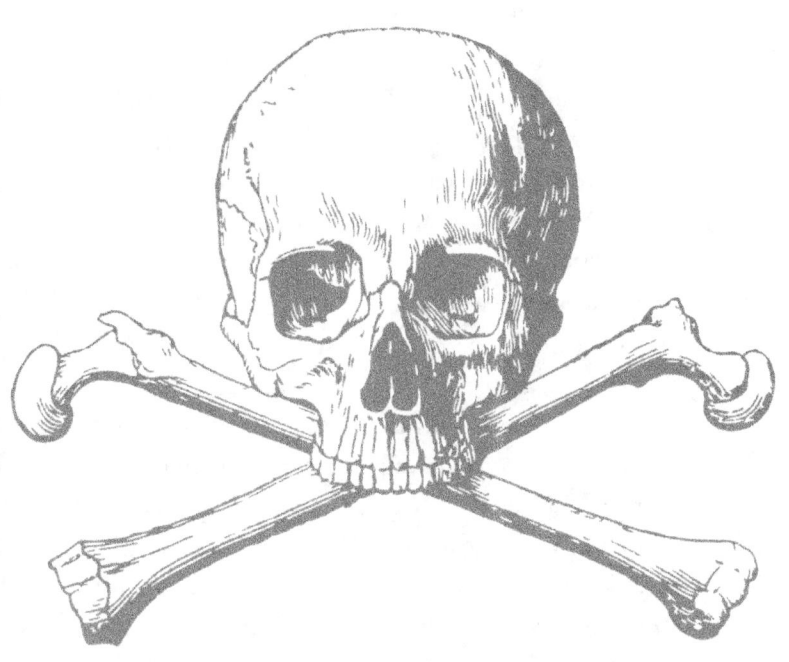

world where death and suffering pre-date the fall of Adam and Eve is to suggest that God's goodness includes such evil. And this we know to be false, for no such equivocal meaning is suggested by God's written revelation. As John C. Whitcomb writes, "a major problem with 'progressive creationism' is its insistence that animals (and even pre-Adamic 'men') died long before Adam had sinned. Thus the strong biblical connection between sin and death is broken."[21]

Ross, and other progressive creationists, hold this view of death pre-existing the historic Adam and Eve, along with many other views (i.e., the theories of the Big Bang, uniformitarianism, etc.), because secular science has reported its supposedly 'unquestionable' findings. But these findings, including those relating to Lyell's theory of uniformitarianism, need to be critically examined for epistemological pre-commitments, that is to say, their religious presuppositions, because no scientific findings can be 'neutral' in relation to the interpretation of God's created evidences.

---

21. Whitcomb, "Progressive Creationism," 2.

Man cannot then engage in 'secular' science, because no science is truly secular. The direction of science conducted by natural men is unavoidably rooted in the religious condition of their hearts. This notion, then, of secular science supplementing our Christian cosmology needs to be corrected if we hope to arrive at a true and right interpretation of reality. And this involves re-directing science towards its true objective, which is to study God's creative handiwork, to interpret created reality after God. It involves, in other words, thinking God's thoughts after Him, in which the written revelation of God serves as the starting point in our thinking. As the late apologist Cornelius Van Til had put it:

> Over against this [autonomous thinking about science] Christianity holds that God is the creator of every fact. There are therefore no brute facts. Thus God's thought is placed back of every fact. Thereby man's thought is made subject to God's thought in the interpretation of every fact. There is not a single

fact that man can interpret rightly without reference to God as the creator of that fact. Man cannot truly apply the category of causality to facts without the presupposition of God. It is God who has caused all facts to stand in a certain relation to one another. Man must seek to discover that relation.[22]

This faithfulness to biblical authority, however, has not been the most prominent trend of the modern Western church. There has, instead, been a departure from the comprehensive scope of God's Word in terms of its interpretation and application, ever since the fall of Christendom. What has taken its place, or filled the void, is a radical dualism which promises better relations with the fallen world, and it promises this by dividing reality into two separate dimensions, the natural (*nature*) and the spiritual (*grace*). Biblical scholars Henry M. and John D. Morris explain how

22. Cornelius Van Til, *Christian Theistic Evidences* (Philadelphia, PA.: Westminster Theological Seminary, 1961), 86.

this plays out: "A popular cliché of neo-orthodox and liberal writers is to the effect that God has revealed in Scripture the *fact* of creation, but has left the *method* of creation to be worked out by scientists."[23] In other words, let the Bible instruct men in their theology, but when it comes to our science, that is best left to natural men. This implies that both the regenerate and the unregenerate can equally learn from one another, as though theologians, operating in the dimension of grace, and scientists, operating in the dimension of nature, were to be on the same 'neutral' ground in their thinking. This completely disregards the sinful orientation of the unregenerate heart, and ignores the worldview differences between the Christian and the natural man. It also shunts the Lordship of Christ to the church instead of the whole world by limiting the scope of God's Word. This promise, it should be noted, of "better relations with the fallen world" always accompanies compromise and apostasy, it is nothing

---

23. Henry M. Morris and John D. Morris, *The Modern Creation Trilogy: Scripture & Creation*, Vol. 1 (Green Forest, AR.: Master Books, 2004), 36.

other than the attempt to dull or blur the antithesis between truth and error, though to do so would be to default to the side of error.

CHAPTER

3

AN EVOLVED EARTH

AS A RESULT OF this departure from biblical authority, progressive creationism, along with other varying perspectives of theistic evolution, which includes orthogenesis, nomogenesis, and emergent evolution, attempted to create a synthesis between the Christian doctrine of creation and naturalistic cosmology.[24] When we consider that naturalists themselves find it difficult to believe that the world and its eco-system came about by purely random natural causes, it is of little surprise that Christians, who adopt a dualistic thinking, have attempted to reconcile the naturalistic origin theses with the Genesis creation narrative. It was, after all, the world-renowned evolutionist Jerry A. Coyne who admitted that, contrary to his naturalistic pre-commitments, "If anything is true about nature, it is that plants and animals seem intricately and almost perfectly *designed* for living their lives."[25]

In order to understand theistic evolution, one must first grasp the naturalist's conception of evolu-

24. Ibid.

25. Jerry A. Coyne, *Why Evolution is True* (Oxford, UK.: Oxford University Press, 2009), 1.

tion as consisting of six components: (i) evolution, (ii) gradualism, (iii) speciation, (iv) common ancestry, (v) natural selection, and (vi) non-selective mechanisms of evolutionary change.[26] Once we grasp these concepts, it is only a matter of supplementing evolutionary theory with theistic elements in order to 'fill in the cracks,' that is to say, to "perfect" the otherwise imperfect cosmology of the naturalist.

We can turn to Coyne's book *Why Evolution is True*, a required textbook for many undergraduate students, for the definition of these six components. The *first component, 'evolution,'* is defined as "a species undergoing genetic change over time... evolv[ing] into something quite different... based on changes in the DNA, which originate as mutations."[27] This concept of evolution as random changes over time is reflective of the overall naturalistic worldview, which not only posits biological evolution, but geological, chemical and cosmological evolution as well; all con-

---

26. Ibid., 3.

27. Ibid.

cepts which the theistic evolutionist adopts. For the purpose of this chapter, however, our scope will be limited to biological evolution.

The second component of evolution, that being *'gradualism,'* is the period of time required for the gradual production of substantial evolutionary change, "such as the evolution of birds from reptiles… usually over hundreds or thousands – even millions – of generations."[28] This concept helps to explain, in part, the diversity of biological life, but it also requires *the third component of evolution*, that of *'speciation.'* The simpler term for this is 'splitting,' which essentially implies the splitting of particular groups from other groups as a result of evolutionary changes, and not simply in regards to appearance, but rather in genetics. In other words, groups that can no longer interbreed with other groups.[29]

This conception of speciation, in turn, implies *the fourth component of evolution, 'common ancestry.'* This

28. Ibid., 4.

29. Ibid., 6.

component is often depicted by a diagram of an evolutionary tree, most famously illustrated by the German biologist Ernst Haeckel (1834-1919), though various modern renditions have since been made. According to naturalists, our supposed common ancestry can be traced through either DNA sequences or the fossil record, a concept that was originally introduced (though not as developed) by Swedish botanist Carl Linnaeus in 1735, prior to Charles Darwin's *On the Origin of Species*.[30] But Darwin followed suit and introduced *the fifth component of evolution*, that is, the process of evolution as *'natural selection.'* In his book, Coyne provides a definition agreeable with theistic evolutionists, the idea of the 'survival of the fittest':

> If individuals within a species differ genetically from one another, and some of those differences affect an individual's ability to survive and reproduce in its environment, then in the next generation the "good" genes that lead to higher survival and re-

---

30. Ibid., 8-9.

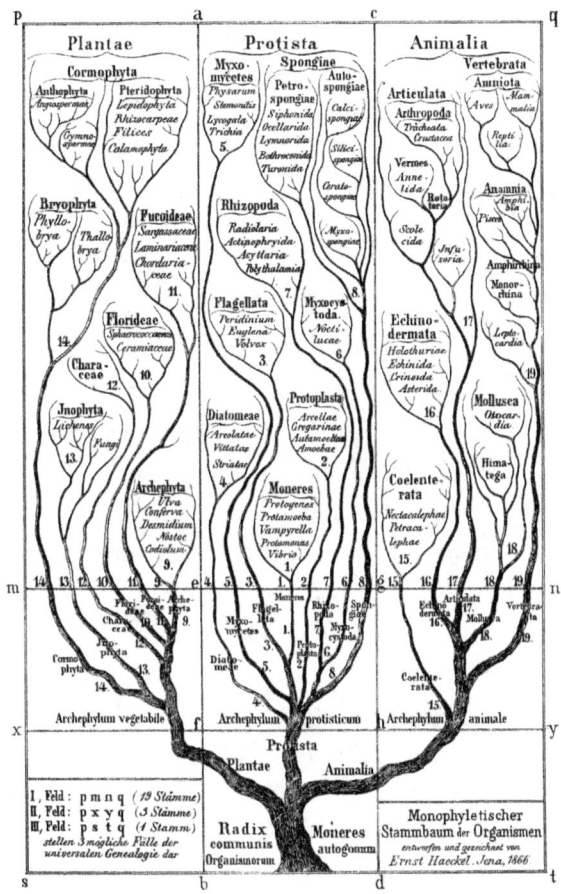

Figure 1: Reproduction of Ernst Haeckel's genealogical tree of life depicting the Kingdoms Plantae (plants), Protista (micro-organisms) and Animalia (animals); Ulrich Kutschera, "From the scala naturae to the symbiogenetic and dynamic tree of life". *Biology Direct.* 6. 33. (2011). 10.1186/1745-6150-6-33.

production will have relatively more copies than the "not so good" genes. Over time, the population will gradually become more and more suited to its environment as helpful mutations arise and spread through the population, while deleterious ones are weeded out.[31]

What follows is *the sixth component of evolution, 'non-selective mechanisms of evolutionary change'*, which, though, not as significant as Darwin's natural selection, or as impactful as common ancestry, is nonetheless integral to the naturalist's understanding of biological evolution, in that there are 'processes other than natural selection' that can cause evolutionary change. This is simply said to be the random changes in the proportion of genes caused by different numbers of offspring, and thus, being random, "has nothing to do with adaptation."[32]

Having laid out the biological evolutionary as-

31. Ibid., 11.
32. Ibid., 14.

pect of the naturalist's cosmology, it is now possible to comprehend and critique the supposed 'Christian' cosmology of theistic evolution. Theistic evolution is nothing more than the dressing up of the originally naturalistic theses in Christian clothing, that is to say, supplementing the gross misinterpretation of God's creation and His evidences with God's authoritative revelation. Note that it is not secular science that supplements Scripture, but Scripture that supplements secular science. Such an act is an outright denial of the sufficiency of Scripture, but given the influence of medieval scholasticism in the modern church, that being the dualism of *nature-grace*, in that *grace* perfects *nature*, and thus Scripture perfects (supplements) the 'natural' sciences – using the apostle Paul's meaning of the word as "unregenerate" (1 Cor. 2:6-16) – this then is not altogether surprising. As a result, the early chapters of Genesis are dismissed as historical and interpreted as either figurative, allegorical, or metaphorical literature;[33] in this manner biblical inerrancy can

33. Wayne Grudem, "Biblical and Theological Introduction" in *Theistic Evolution: A Scientific, Philosophical and*

49

be supposedly 'preserved' while the natural, secular scientists are revered as the ultimate epistemological authority, which is nothing else but the pretended autonomy of man. As the late apologist Greg L. Bahnsen defined it:

> "Autonomy" refers to being a law unto oneself, so that one's thinking is independent of any outside authority, including God's. Autonomous reasoning takes itself philosophically as the final point of reference and interpretation, the ultimate court of intellectual appeal; it presumes to be self-governing, self-determinative, and self-directing.[34]

The three most popular formulations of theistic evolution are: (i) *orthogenesis*, the belief that God directed the mutation/selection mechanism, that is, the

---

Theological Critique, eds. J.P. Moreland, Stephen C. Meyer, Christopher Shaw, Ann K. Gauger, and Wayne Grudem (Wheaton, IL: Crossway, 2017), 65.

34. Greg L. Bahnsen, *Van Til's Apologetic: Readings & Analysis* (Phillipsburg, NJ.: P&R Publishing, 1998), 1.

biological evolutionary process; (ii) *nomogenesis*, the belief that God merely designed the laws of nature in order that nature might bring about the origin and development of life. In other words, the universe is a self-sustaining mechanism, operating independently of God. And (iii) *an amended form of nomogenesis*, in which God created the laws of nature, but also upholds these laws on a moment-by-moment basis. In exception of the first formulation, the latter two essentially imply that, according to geophysicist Stephen C. Meyer:

> ...the mechanisms of natural selection and random mutation (and/or other similarly undirected evolutionary mechanisms) are... the main causal actor(s) in producing new forms of life. Thus, God does not act directly or "intervene" within the orderly concourse of nature.[35]

The implications of adopting either of these two

---

35. Stephen C. Meyer, "Scientific and Philosophical Introduction," in *Theistic Evolution*, 44.

views, which contradict the Scriptural teaching of God's creation of the universe in six days (Gen. 1-2) and His sustaining of the entire cosmos (Acts 17:28; 1 Cor. 8:6; Col. 1:17; Heb. 1:3), is the inevitable development of a worldview foreign to that of Scripture. To be more precise, it is to adopt the worldview of deism, where god is altogether distant and uninvolved with the created cosmos.[36] This conception of "god" is antithetical to the doctrine of God in Scripture, for while Scripture teaches a logically consistent distinction between Creator and creation, deism deifies and absolutizes nature given the supposed absence of the Creator. And if man can dominate and control nature, then man can be deified; it is the humanistic ground-motive of deism. This deification of nature, whether explicitly recognized or not, yields itself to a Oneist worldview where there is no Creator-creation distinction, which by implication should render all distinctions within creation distinction-less. It can be rightly said with confidence then, that to be a deist is

36. Ibid., 45.

to not be a Christian, for Scripture has ceased to be an authoritative foundation, and thus a deistic interpretation of Genesis 1-3 is at odds, not only with the Hebrew and Christian understanding of the texts, but with God's written revelation about Himself and the world.

However, the first formulation of theistic evolution is what is most championed in Christian circles because of its (i) claim to avoid the false concept of deism, and its (ii) affirmation of the Bible as God's special, authoritative revelation. BioLogos, for example, a theistic evolutionist advocacy group, claims that it:

> ...presents the Evolutionary Creationism (EC) viewpoint on origins. Like all Christians, we fully affirm that God is the creator of all life – including human beings in his image. We fully affirm that the Bible is the inspired and authoritative word of God. We also accept the science of evolution as the best description for how God brought about the

diversity of life on earth.[37]

What BioLogos means by "creator of all life" is that God created matter in the beginning with "certain physical properties and then the properties of matter were enough to bring about all living things" with the direction and intervention of God.[38] This means that God did not create Adam and Eve from the dust, not literally as the text suggests, but rather that they were merely products of biological evolution, originating from a primordial common ancestor that unites all biological life forms. There were then, at the time, a few thousands of hominids, and Adam and Eve were amongst them. As the theologian Wayne Grudem affirms, "those Christians who support theistic evolution and also want to retain belief in a historical Adam and Eve propose that God chose one

37. "How is BioLogos Different from Evolutionism, Intelligent Design, and Creationism?" *BioLogos*, http://biologos.org/common-questions/christianity-and-science/biologos-id-creationism/.

38. Grudem, "Biblical and Theological Introduction" in *Theistic Evolution*, 68.

man and one woman from the thousands… who were living on the earth."[39]

This first formulation of theistic evolution is just as antithetical to Scripture as the latter two, however, as it contradicts the clear witness of God's written revelation as laid out in Table 1: A Comparison of Theistic Evolution & Biblical Creationism.

A theistic evolutionist would need to be consistent with what he believes cosmologically if he hopes to understand the incongruence and incompatibility between evolution and biblical doctrine. The evolutionary process, for example, is centred around survival. The strong and fertile organisms, in terms of their ability to adapt to their environments, survive and thrive to be the dominant species, while the week and feeble are weeded out to the extent of extinction. If man is the by-product of evolution, and man is the crown of God's creation (as a result of being created in the *imago Dei*), then the chief good of evolution is

---

39. Ibid., 69.

Theistic Evolution	Biblical Creationism
Adam and Eve were not the first human beings.	Adam and Eve were the first human beings, and thus representatives of the human race (Gen. 1:26-30).
Adam and Eve were born from human parents.	Adam and Eve were created by God, no humans preceded them (Gen. 2:4-7).
God did not create Adam and Eve from the non-living materials of the earth.	Adam and Eve were created from the non-living materials of the earth (Gen 2:7; 3:19).
God did not create Eve from the rib of Adam.	Eve was created from the rib of Adam (Gen. 2:20-23).
Adam and Eve were not sinless creatures.	Adam and Eve were originally righteous and sinless (Gen. 1:27).
Adam and Eve did not commit the first sin.	Adam and Eve, as the first parents of the human race, committed the first sin (Gen. 3).

Death and suffering were not caused by the curse laid upon creation because of Adam and Eve's sin.	Death and suffering entered the world because of Adam and Eve's sin (Gen. 3:16-19; Rom. 8:20).
Not all humans are descendants of Adam and Eve.	All human beings are descendants of Adam and Eve (Gen. 5).
God did not create 'kinds,' but rather a biological organism, through which he diversified the whole eco-system.	God created each animal according to their "kinds" (Gen. 1:20-25).
God did not rest from His creation but is still guiding/directing the evolutionary process.	God rested from His creation work on the seventh day, while still sustaining the universe (Gen. 2:1-3; Col. 1:17).
God did not create an originally good natural world.	God created an originally "very good" natural world (Gen. 1:31).
No curse was laid upon the creation of God as a result of Adam and Eve's sin.	A curse was laid upon the creation of God as a result of Adam and Eve's sin (Gen. 3:16-19).

Table 1: A Comparison of Theistic Evolution & Biblical Creationism

struggle and survival.[40] But this is contrary to the character of the biblical God, who established an objective ethical system which contradicts this notion of the survival of the fittest. By Darwinian standards, we are to weed out the sick, the disabled, the most genetically flawed (to slow down our genetic entropy) by concentrating our medical and social resources towards those who seem much worthier, those most suitable for the preservation of the human race. But Scripture teaches that we are all created in the image of God, and as a result, the sick are to be tended to, the disabled taken care of, and the outcasts reintegrated into society.[41] What reason could be given by the theistic evolutionist for the care of man, whether it be a suitable specimen for the preservation and procreation of the human race, or an outcast, when evolution teaches

40. Morris and Morris, *The Modern Creation Trilogy*, Vol. 1, 39.

41. Carlisle Percival, "The Imago Dei in Modern Healthcare," in *Jubilee: Recovering Biblical Foundations for Our Time*, ed. Joseph Boot, Spring 2010 (Toronto, ON.: Ezra Institute for Contemporary Christianity, 2010), 14.

the survival of the self above all else? On this basis, all human rights declarations should be discarded as they obstruct nature's natural process of eliminating the weak, and rewarding the strong. In the biblical system of ethics, however, we find there reflected the moral righteousness and perfection of God, and the grace and mercy that He has bestowed upon created man. Whereas evolution revolves around the survival of the fittest, Christian theism revolves around the sacrifice of oneself for another, as supremely exemplified in the redemptive work of Jesus Christ.[42] In truth, the structure of Western law and human rights was originally built on a Christian *ethos* that was once prominent in society, owing nothing to evolutionary thought.

We must take note of the fact that the implications of positing theistic evolution as *the* Christian cosmology are radical, for it implies, for example, that the God of life is in actuality the god of death. This is not what we read in Scripture at all, for as Job

---

42. Morris and Morris, *The Modern Creation Trilogy*, Vol. 1, 39.

says, "You have granted me life and lovingkindness; and Your care has preserved my spirit" (Job 10:12). This radical departure from the God of life, however, is rooted in the evolutionary process, which requires the death of millions of organisms in order to arrive at the end by-products of evolution as God's "very good" creation. This process, whether the theistic evolutionist recognizes or not, implies God's powerlessness, for if Scripture teaches that He is omnipotent (Isa. 14:27), and fully capable of creating the universe in an instant, then why did it require eons of time in order to create the cosmos?[43] Why was it such a painful, grueling long process? And by implication, God's personality should also be questioned, for why did God wait until the latter end of geologic time before creating personalities? It appears as though there was great difficulty in creating personalities according to the evolutionary timeline, which is contrary to the clear witness of Scripture (Gen. 1:25-28).[44] We also

43. Ibid., 39.

44. Ibid., 40.

read throughout the Bible of God's omniscience, for as the Creator and Lord over all, He knows all things past, present and future (Isa. 46:9-10). And yet, according to the theistic evolutionist, the fossil record testifies of God's failed evolutionary mutations, being riddled with extinction events and supposed biological misfits.[45] Was the creative work of God built upon prior failed experiments? Did God not 'know it all' after all? If we evaluate these radical implications and consider what Scripture teaches on God's sovereignty, H. and J. Morris write that:

> If God's purpose was the creation and redemption of man, as theistic evolutionists presumably believe, it seems incomprehensible that He would waste billions of years in aimless evolutionary meandering before getting to the point.[46]

In other words, where the literal interpretation of Genesis makes clear the purpose of God in His prov-

45. Ibid.

46. Ibid.

idential work, the evolutionary theory reduces Him to aimlessness. These are only but a few of the implications of theistic evolution, but they are reflective of the fact that changes to the biblical cosmology not only affect certain aspects of God's character and attributes, but affect the whole doctrine of God. The god of theistic evolutionism, then, can be characterized as a cruel, capricious god of suffering and death. He is not omnipotent, nor omniscient, or even anywhere close to morally upright. He falls short of a personal or relational being, and as evident in the evolutionary process, is void of all overarching purpose. This is not the God of the Bible, and this is not the God of Genesis. Thus, the god of theistic evolution is an entirely different god, a false idol, crafted and shaped by the vain thoughts of man, according to the patterns of this world (Rom. 12:2). But theistic evolutionists are not the only "Christians" who commit this gross error; progressive creationists are in the same boat, suffering the same radical implications.[47] It is the inevi-

47. Ibid., 41.

table result of distorting God's Word by reading man's unregenerate thought into the text. As a result, both alternative interpretations of progressive creationism and theistic evolution are to be discarded in our answer to the question of origins.

CHAPTER

4

A FUNCTIONAL
EARTH

THE THIRD ALTERNATIVE to the interpretation of the biblical creation narrative is 'ancient cosmology,' what can be rightly discerned to be a smokescreen or diversion tactic, considering that it diverts our attention from the intended literal meaning of the text and towards a different, more obscure focus or perspective. This interpretation is posited in order that the door might be left open to various cosmological origin theses, one being, for example, the "evolutionist's foot in the door" as it might be said. Several interpretations fall within this category, such as the Framework Hypothesis, which regards Genesis as a mere literary device while dismissing its historical value,[48] and the Gap Theory, which attempts to cram millions of years in-between the first two verses of Genesis 1.[49] However, the most prominent and novel of these is Walton's *functional framework*, here on referred to as 'functionalism.'

---

48. See Sarfati, *Refuting Compromise*, 94-101.

49. See Morris and Morris, *The Modern Creation Trilogy,* Vol. 1, 50-59.

Walton, a self-professed theistic evolutionist,[50] makes no attempt to distort the text of Genesis to fit the cosmological origins proposed by secular science, but rather posits an *altogether different reading* of Genesis, one which compliments biological, geological, chemical and cosmological evolution. This he calls 'ancient cosmology,' regarding Genesis, not as a historical document as modernly understood, but as a form of communicating history that is unfamiliar to 21st century minds. He puts it this way, "The problem is, we cannot translate their cosmology to our cosmology, nor should we."[51] The reason for this is that God could not have revealed a science to the Hebrews that was beyond their culture, or that He could not have communicated a language beyond their primitiveness, but Walton falsely assumes that the literal interpreta-

---

50. See John D. Currid, "Theistic Evolution is Incompatible with the Teachings of the Old Testament" in *Theistic Evolution*, 843.

51. John H. Walton, *The Lost World of Genesis One: Ancient Cosmology and the Origins Debate* (Downers Grove, IL.: IVP Academic, 2009), 14-15.

tion of Genesis renders the text a scientific account of cosmological origins, or an account that goes way over the heads of the original recipients. This could not be farther from the truth. The opening chapters of Genesis are not scientific, they are historical, and as such they have scientific implications. This fact Walton does not understand, instead, he regards the text as either 'ancient cosmology' or as a scientific text of modernity, and because of the impossibility of the latter, it must be the former. There are in fact other options, but Walton firmly believes that God's progressive revelation is limited by the primitive nature of mankind.

Thus, this ancient cosmology, according to Walton, does not provide an account of material origins. Instead, it provides an account of God's assignment of functions to different elements of the material universe. This means that the "actual creative act is to assign something its functional role in the ordered system... an ordered system in human terms, that is, relation to society and culture."[52] It is, therefore, an

52. Ibid., 24-25.

anthropocentric reading of the text, where all created things serve some purpose or function in relation to human life and culture.

The assignment of functions to God's creation cannot be denied. After all, God created all things with a divine purpose in mind, and so in this regard, we can thank Walton for highlighting the relation of created things to the image bearer, and how creation might serve as a cosmic temple that glorifies God. However, Walton wanders beyond the confines of the text by *over-emphasizing* the assignment of roles and functions in his thesis, forcefully confining the meaning of the text to functionalism, and dismissing material origins altogether from the narrative.[53] In other words, Walton proposes that Genesis 1-2 is more about the assignment of roles and functions than any real, literal history of God's material creation.

In his review of Walton's thesis, biblical scholar

---

53. Currid, "Theistic Evolution is Incompatible with the Teachings of the Old Testament," in *Theistic Evolution*, 851.

Vern S. Poythress notes that Walton's definition and use of the word 'material' is far too ambiguous, and as a result of his reading into the text, he has constructed an unbiblical dualistic worldview:

> The word "material" can denote material composition or physical appearance or both together. The "material" composition of a college building is the concrete, wiring, piping, and other pieces that make up its structure. The "material" (physical appearance) for a college is the buildings, landscaping, and parking lots that compose its campus. We can describe a college on at least three levels, (1) its material composition, (2) its physical appearance, and (3) its human purpose of learning... Dr. Walton and I agree that Genesis 1 does not address area #1, material composition. We also agree that it does have information about services to human beings (#3). The difficulty arises with area #2, physical appearances.

For example, I believe that Genesis 1:9 implies that dry land appeared. Likewise, Genesis 1:11-12 implies that plants appear on the land.... [Walton] implies that they have nothing to say about the "material" aspect... if it includes only human services (3) and not appearances (2), we are not in agreement.[54]

Walton has read Genesis with a false contrast between material and functional, and with equivocal meanings for the two terms... As a result, he artificially detaches Genesis 1 from questions of physical appearance and produces an unsustainable interpretation.[55]

54. Vern S. Poythress, "Vern Poythress Responds to John Walton," *BioLogos*, accessed December 08, 2017. https://biologos.org/blogs/archive/vern-poythress-responds-to-john-walton/.

55. Poythress, "Appearances Matter: Author presents a false contrast between the material and functional in Genesis," *WORLD Magazine*, accessed December 11, 2017. https://world.mng.org/2009/08/appearances_matter/.

This unbiblical dualism of Walton's functionalism is the division of the material and the functional, as if the one were to be a completely separate layer of reality from the other, that being (i) the physical appearance of the cosmos, and (ii) individual purpose and temple consecration.[56] This duality provides no room for overlap, according to Walton's thesis; as a result they are irreconcilable and completely independent from one another.

Walton fails to comprehend that this *material-functional* paradigm is just another offspring manifestation of the *nature-grace* dualism of scholastic thought, likened to the division of the *secular* (material) and the *sacred* (functions), which runs contrary to the biblical paradigm of *creation-fall-redemption*, that is, the restoration of the whole created order from its state of corruption in terms of the proclamation and advancement of the kingdom of God. The biblical paradigm does not commit the error of dualistic thinking, it does not divide reality into two separate

---

56. Poythress, "Vern Poythress Responds to John Walton."

layers, the material and the functional. It instead testifies that all created material is inseparable from its created function, for how can one exist without the other? No such *nature-grace* (spiritual) dualism can be read into the Scriptures when God's written revelation affirms the unity of the material and the functional, the natural and the spiritual, in God's whole created order.

To interpret Genesis according to the functionalism of Walton is to outright ignore the historical traits of the Genesis creation narrative, to run contrary to the faithful historic interpretation of the church by positing an altogether novel thesis[57] with poor exegesis,[58] and to cause the same violence to the biblical

---

57. N.T. Wright, in "Product Description: Review," *Amazon.ca*, accessed December 08, 2017. https://www.amazon.ca/Lost-World-of-Genesis-John-Walton/dp/0830837043/.

58. A comparison of Walton's exegesis in *The Lost World of Genesis One* with other conservative exegetical commentaries reveals the extent of his eisegesis according to his pre-commitment to the idea of 'ancient cosmology.' It

doctrine of God as both progressive creationism and theistic evolution. This distortion of the truth is always to be expected when the written revelation of God is not accepted as it is – when man decides, according to his own pretended autonomy, to conform Scripture to his own presuppositions, instead of allowing it to transform his understanding of reality.

---

should be noted that a proper exegesis involves adopting the same presuppositions of Scripture, and allowing said presuppositions to challenge our interpretative thinking.

CHAPTER

5

THE SELF-WITNESS OF
SCRIPTURE

AS WE BEAR THESE cosmological origin alternatives in mind, we need to be reminded that, though the Bible is not a scientific textbook, it is nonetheless propositional revelation, that is to say, it makes clear to us true propositions, or facts about things, in intelligible human words. The Bible is, given its divine inspiration, an authoritative written interpretation of God's general revelation in creation. And as such, it is therefore subject to grammatical rules and historical context.[59] This means that we can study God's Word and understand it linguistically and historically, including its claim that God created the universe in six days, and, according to the recorded genealogies, a few thousands of years ago.

The fact is that, if we affirm the inspiration, inerrancy and sufficiency of Scripture, then as it concerns the study of our natural world and its origin, we have no other place to go but to the Bible, for only through its worldview lens can we make sense of our created reality. This involves consulting Scripture on what it

---

59. Sarfati, *Refuting Compromise*, 35.

claims about its own creation account, that is, its own interpretation of Genesis 1-3. How did the prophets and apostles under the Spirit of God and the Lord Jesus Christ regard the creation narrative? Did they regard it as literal, figurative, archetypical, or symbolic? The answer, as made evident in the following passages, is that of a literal interpretation:

> Remember the Sabbath day, to keep it holy. Six days you shall labor, and do all your work, but the seventh day is a Sabbath to the LORD your God. On it you shall not do any work, you, or your son, or your daughter, your male servant, or your female servant, or your livestock, or the sojourner who is within your gates. *For in six days the LORD made heaven and earth, the sea, and all that is in them, and rested on the seventh day.* Therefore the LORD blessed the Sabbath day and made it holy (Exodus 20:8-11).

> It is a sign forever between me and the people of Israel that in *six days the LORD made*

heaven and earth, and on the seventh day he rested and was refreshed (Exodus 31:17).

By *the word of the Lord* the heavens were made, and *by the breath of his mouth* all their host (Psalm 33:6).

Ah, Lord God! It is you who have *made the heavens and the earth* by your great power and outstretched arm. Nothing is too hard for you (Jeremiah 32:17).

He answered, "Have you not read that *he who created them from the beginning made them male and female*, and said, 'Therefore a man shall leave his father and his mother and hold fast to his wife, and the two shall become one flesh'? So they are no longer two but one flesh. What therefore God has joined together, let not man separate" (Matthew 19:4-6).

Jesus, when he began his ministry, was about thirty years of age, being the son (as

81

was supposed) of Joseph, the son of Heli, the son of Matthat, the son of Levi, the son of Melchi, the son of Jannai, the son of Joseph... the son of Cainan, the son of Arphaxad, the son of Shem, the son of Noah, the son of Lamech... the son of Enos, the son of Seth, *the son of Adam, the son of God* (Luke 3:23-38).

Scripture explicitly regards the opening chapters of Genesis as history. There is not a single passage from Genesis to Revelation that suggests that Genesis should be taken, even in part, as poetic, allegorical, or symbolic. To deny the historicity of Genesis 1-3 is to leave the rest of God's written revelation without a foundation, for it is made clear that God created the universe perfectly good (*tov*), in six days, and that His creation was subjected to futility when humanity's first parents fell from their original righteousness (Rom. 8:20). The entire redemptive narrative of Scripture would mean nothing if not for the opening chapters of Genesis, for what redemption could there be if sin could not be accounted for?

This biblical understanding, then, of God's creation in Genesis 1-2 means that death and suffering could not have preceded the creation of Adam and Eve. Instead, life and perfect health was what characterized the pre-fall world, up until the events of Genesis 3. This is what Scripture teaches, for Paul wrote to the Romans that "sin came into the world through one man, and death through sin, and so death spread to all men because all sinned" (Rom. 5:12; Cf. 5:12-19), and to the Corinthians, "For as by a man came death, by a man has come also the resurrection of the dead. For as in Adam all die, so also in Christ shall all be made alive" (1 Cor. 15:21-22). Remove the historical creation narrative, or remove the historical Adam, and you are left without the doctrines of sin and redemption, and a false contrast between Adam and Christ; these passages would effectually be rendered meaningless and void.

In truth, it would be illogical to posit that death pre-existed the creation of mankind when Paul refers to death "as the last enemy to be defeated" in God's great unfolding plan of redemptive and restorative history (1 Cor. 15:26). And that is what death is, an enemy of God, an opposing force that will be vanquished from creation upon the consummation of all things (Rev. 21:4). This, of course, raises questions as to the facts and evidences of our natural world, for how does the Christian then make sense of the millions of dead organisms found in the fossil record?

If Scripture provides no room for the Gap Theory, and if there was no such geological uniformitarian timeline, then what does Scripture teach that might help us in our interpretation of our created world? The answer to this question can be found in the account of the post-fall, global flood of Noah's day (Gen. 6-9), when God poured out His judgment upon the earth for mankind's wickedness. This historical event communicated to us that the whole of creation suffers when those who have been given dominion over the earth rebel against their Creator. And, as a result, the fossil record now serves as a testament to man of

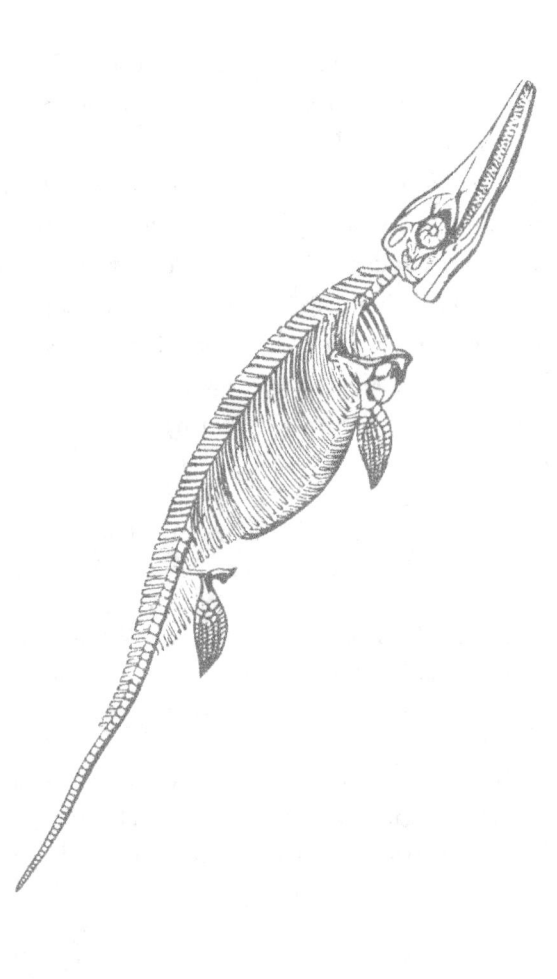

his own sinfulness, and of God's righteous judgment which never fails; it also affirms the biblical timeline and the written revelation of God, for what we expect to see is in fact what we find, that is, millions of dead organisms buried in rock layers all around the world.[60] Ken Ham, founder of Answers in Genesis, writes here that the Genesis flood "has made the earth's geology, geography, biology, etc., what they are today... the global devastation caused by Noah's Flood must therefore have a part in any explanation of the fossil record."[61]

---

60. A more comprehensive study of the flood and the fossil record are provided in Henry M. Morris' and John C. Whitcomb's *The Genesis Flood*, John Woodmorappe's *Noah's Ark: A Feasibility Study*, and Andrew Snelling's two volumes of *Earth's Catastrophic Past*, all which are arguably the most definitive publications on the subject matter.

61. Ken Ham, "Creation, Flood and Coming Fire," Answers in Genesis, accessed December 1, 2017. https://answersingenesis.org/bible-history/creation-flood-and-coming-fire/.

Scripture, therefore, interprets its own creation narrative as literal history, but how can we be sure of its interpretation? Might presupposing literalism be considered another form of eisegesis as we deal with the text? Eisegesis occurs whenever the reader imposes his or her own interpretation onto the text, what always happens when the very same presuppositions of Scripture are disregarded, but exegesis differs in that it is the drawing out of the meaning from the text in accordance with the context and meaning of the author. It is the purity of the exegesis, that is, its faithfulness to the testimony of Scripture, and its honest transparency in its dealing with the text, which ultimately makes clear the true, objective interpretation.

CHAPTER

6

HERMENEUTICS
APPLIED

FOR THE CREATION NARRATIVE, we can turn to a word study and a literary analysis of Genesis 1, beginning with the Hebrew word *yom,* which has caused the most division in its interpretation. The semantic range of *yom,* translated as "day," is restricted to only five meanings:[62]

1. A period of light in a day/night cycle;
2. A period of 24 hours;
3. A general or vague concept of time;
4. A specific point of time; and
5. A period of a year.

As to what meaning is ascribed to *yom* in Genesis 1-3, the answer is found in its literary context.

The genre of Genesis is historical, not poetic or allegorical.[63] If the book of Genesis, and this includes the beginning chapters (1-11), were to be compared

---

62. Sarfati, *Refuting Compromise,* 67-68.
63. Sarfati, *The Genesis Account: A Theological, Historical and Scientific Commentary on Genesis 1-11* (Powder Springs, GA.: Creation Book Publishers, 2015), 34.

to the other historical books of the Old Testament, such as Exodus, Numbers, Joshua, etc., it would be evident that the same literary style is employed by its author. Sarfati, in his *Commentary on Genesis*, writes that "Genesis frequently uses the construction called the '*waw* consecutive' (or *wayyiqtol* or *preterite*), a singular mark of sequential narrative,"[64] which is in fact a common trait of ancient Hebraic history.[65] Sarfati also notes "other trademarks of historical narrative, such as 'accusative particles' ('*et*) that mark the objects of verbs, and many terms that are carefully defined."[66] These other "trademarks" include Hebrew verbs exhibiting features that are expected for recounting past historical events, where, for example, *bara* (create) is *qatal*, and subsequent verbs are *wayyiqtols*, forming the sequentiality of the narrative. This is affirmed by German Hebraist H.F. Wilhelm Gesenius (1786-

64. Ibid., 48.

65. See J. Weingreen, *A Practical Grammar for Classical Hebrew* (Oxford, UK.: Oxford University Press, 1967), 90-92.

66. Sarfati, *The Genesis Account*, 48.

1842), who wrote:

> One of the most striking peculiarities in the Hebrew *consecution* of tenses is the phenomenon that, in representing a series of past events, only the first verb stands in the perfect, and the narration is continued in the imperfect.[67]

The very notion of Genesis 1-3 being in any form poetic or allegorical is contrary to the clear literary style of the text, most particularly considering the absence of parallelism which is common in poetic Hebrew literature. Though it is true that the creation narrative has a repetitive structure which can be confused for poetry, consisting of (1) God's command, (2) its fulfillment, (3) its assessment, and (4) the closure of the day, there is no literary or historical evidence that would suggest that this text is non-historical.[68] In fact,

---

67. Heinrich Friedrich Wilhelm Gesenius, *Gesenius' Hebrew Grammar*, 2nd edition, trans. Arthur Ernest Cowley (Oxford, UK.: Oxford University Press, 1910), 132-133.

68. Sarfati, *The Genesis Account*, 50-51.

such repetition is a common literary device for the memorization of *oral traditions*.

Also consider that the words *boqer* (morning) and *erebs* (evening) denotes a literal day; and contrary to those who claim that these are 'figurative' terms, outside of Genesis 1, these words are combined with *yom* for a total of nineteen times, always meaning a literal day.[69] Even without the word *yom*, the words *boqer* and *erebs* together always mean a 24-hour period, and this occurs "38 times outside of Genesis 1, including 25 in historical narrative."[70] Essentially, when comparing the word usage of *yom* (day) with other biblical passages (i.e, Num. 9:15; Deut. 16:4; Dan. 8:26), particularly when accompanied by a number, or by the Hebrew words *boqer* and *erebs*, it can only mean "an ordinary day, never a long period of time," according to Safarti.[71]

When we consider all these indicators, the word

---

69. Sarfati, *Refuting Compromise*, 81.

70. Ibid.

71. Ibid., 67.

usage and meanings of *yom*, *boqer*, and *erebs*, the literary genre and accompanying literary devices, the absence of allegorical or figurative language, and the fact that the Hebrews used what words they could in the understanding of their day to describe the comprehensiveness of God's creative work (v. 1, "God created the heavens and the earth")[72], it is abundantly clear that to deny the historical and literal nature of Genesis would be to deny the obvious meaning of the text. And if any attempt were made to 'extract' a meaning that is otherwise different than the intended meaning of the text, not only should we evaluate the underlying motives for that person's distortion of God's Word, but be weary of the fact that such an attempt would cause structural and directional damage to the rest of our understanding of Scripture.

It is only by interpreting the Genesis creation narrative according to the testimony of Scripture, and according to hermeneutical principles which uphold biblical authority, that we can affirm the true attri-

---

72. Currid, "The Hebrew World-and-Life View," 51.

butes and character of God. This being the holiness, justice, omnipotence, omniscience, perfection, truthfulness, goodness, sovereignty, transcendence, providence and mercy of the personal, creator God. And it is precisely this that we see reflected in the Genesis creation narrative, for as H. and J. Morris write:

> Surely an omniscient God [would] devise a better process of creation than the random, wasteful, inefficient trial-and-error charade of the so-called geological ages, and certainly a loving, merciful God would never be guilty of a creative process that would involve the suffering and death of multitudes of innocent animals in the process of arriving at man millions of years later.[73]

The original state of creation reflected the goodness of God, goodness in terms of God's law-word, and it is precisely because of the goodness of God that creation will be restored to its original state again.

---

73. Morris and Morris, *The Modern Creation Trilogy*, Vol. 1, 76.

John Calvin (1509-1564), the Genevan reformer, wrote in relation to the goodness of God and creation that God pronounced His creation as "perfectly good, that we may know that there is in the symmetry of God's works the highest perfection, to which nothing can be added."[74] Matthew Henry (1662-1714), the puritan, also commented that:

> The work of creation was a very good work. All that God made was well-made, and there was no flaw nor defect in it.... Good, for it is all agreeable to the mind of the Creator, just as he would have it be... Good, for it is all for God's glory; there is that in the whole visible creation which is a demonstration of God's being and perfections...[75]

---

74. John Calvin, *Genesis*, 1554 (Edinburgh, UK.: Banner of Truth, 1984), 100.

75. Matthew Henry, *Matthew Henry's Commentary on the Whole Bible: Complete and Unabridged in One Volume* (Peabody: Hendrickson, 1994), 7.

CHAPTER

7

PATRISTIC
COMMENTARIES

AS DIFFICULT AS IT MAY be to believe, both progressive creationists and theistic evolutionists argue that the literal six-day, young-earth interpretation is a novel, reactionary development to the more recent 'scientific' understanding of natural origins, and that, as it relates to history, the early church fathers sided with an old-earth interpretation as opposed to the supposedly 'modern' reactionary creationism.[76] As Mook elaborates, "They propose that prominent early Church exegetes pursued *theological* meaning as of the highest priority (rather than historical meaning), and

76. Ross, for example, stated that "Many of the early church fathers and other Biblical scholars interpreted the creation days Genesis 1 as long periods of time. The list of such proponents includes the Jewish historian Josephus (1st century); Irenaeus, bishop of Lyons, apologist, and martyr (2nd century); Origen, who rebutted heathen attacks on Christian doctrine (3rd century); Basil (4th century); Augustine (5th century); and, later, Aquinas (13th century), to name a few" in "Biblical Evidence for Long Creation Days", *Reasons.org*, 1 December 2002.; See also Sarfati, "Hugh Ross Church Fathers: Old earther admits 'poor quality' research by other old-earthers," *Creation.com*. Accessed November 30, 2017. https://creation.com/hugh-ross-church-fathers/.

would not [thus] identify with modern young-earth theses."[77]

This notion, however, of the literal, six-day interpretation of Genesis 1-2 as "novel" and "reactionary" is not only false but a scholarly embarrassment.[78] Though it is true that naturalism dates back to ancient Greek philosophy, with Hippasus, Anaximander, Thales the Milesian, and Xenophanes, teaching that all things originated from a single entity (fire, air, water, or earth), the early church patristics rejected said naturalism in their theology of cosmological origins.[79] Hippolytus (c. AD 170-235), a presbyter of Rome, for example, cites and rejects many of these Greek nat-

77. Mook, "The Church Fathers on Genesis, the Flood, and the Age of the Earth," in *Coming to Grips with Genesis*, 25.

78. See Don Stoner, *A New Look at an Old Earth* (Eugene, OR.: Harvest House Publishers, 1997), 37-41.

79. Hippolytus, *Refutation of all Heresies* 10.2, in Alexander Roberts, James Donaldson, Philip Schaff, Henry Wace, eds., *The Ante-Nicene Fathers*, 10 vols. (Peabody, MA.: Hendrickson, 1994), vol. 5.

uralistic teachings in his book *Refutation of all Heresies*.[80]

The Bishop Basil of Caesarea (AD 329-379) likewise rejected the naturalism of the Greeks, stating:

> Some had recourse to material principles and attributed the origin of the Universe to the elements of the world... A true spider's web woven by these writers who give to heaven, to earth, and to sea so weak an origin and so little consistency!... Deceived by their inherent atheism it appeared to them that nothing governed or ruled the universe, and that all was given up to chance.[81]

Both progressive and biblical creationists may agree with St. Basil's assessment, after all, both reject the atheistic worldview, but this is as far as the

---

80. Ibid., 10.2-10.3

81. Basil of Caesarea, *Hexaemeron* 1.2 in Alexander Roberts, James Donaldson, Philip Schaff, Henry Wace, eds., *The Nicene and Post-Nicene Fathers, Series 2* (Peabody, MA.: Hendrickson, 1994) vol. 8.

agreement goes, for the patristics go on to state their interpretations of the Genesis creation narrative as 'creation in six literal days and as not that long ago.' Lactantius (AD 250-325), for example, advisor to the Roman Emperor Constantine I and tutor of his son, wrote that the naturalistic philosophers, those "who enumerate thousands of ages from the beginning of the world, [should] know that the six thousandth year is not yet completed... God completed the world and this admirable work of nature in the space of six days."[82] The bishop Victorinus of Pettau (c. AD 304) taught that each day of creation was divided into twelve hours of daylight and twelve hours of night, stating "God produced that entire mass for the adornment of His majesty in six days; on the seventh to which He consecrated it."[83] And one of the few patristics who mastered the Hebrew language, Ephrem the Syrian (c. AD 306-373), wrote: "So let no one think

82. Lactantius, *Institutes* 7.14, in *The Ante-Nicene Fathers*, vol. 7.

83. Victorinus, *On the Creation of the World*, in *The Ante-Nicene Fathers*, vol. 7, 341.

that there is anything allegorical in the works of the six days. No one can rightly say that the things pertaining to these days were symbolic."[84]

Now, it may well be countered that these citations were of the patristic literalists, but what about the allegorists? Perhaps they held to a "day-age" perspective on cosmological origins. Not quite. In fact, Origen (c. AD 185-254) wrote that "the Mosaic account of creation… teaches that the world is not yet ten thousand years old, but very much under that."[85] His predecessor, the head of the Catechetical School of Alexandria, St. Clement (c. AD 150-211), wrote: "For the creations on the different days followed in a most important succession; so that all things brought into existence might have honor from priority, created

---

84. Ephrem the Syrian, *Commentary on Genesis* 1.1, in Kathleen E. McVey, ed., *Ephrem the Syrian: Selected Prose Works*, trans. Edward G. Mathews and Joseph P. Amar, in *The Fathers of the Church* (Washington, DC.: Catholic Univ. of Amer. Pr., 1961), 91:74.

85. Origen, *De Principiis* 1.19, in *The Ante-Nicene Fathers*, vol. 4.

together in thought…"[86] Mook, in his contributing chapter to the book *Coming to Grips with Genesis*, collects the citations of various patristics to demonstrate that these aforementioned fathers, and others such as Athanasius,[87] St. Augustine,[88] and Ambrose,[89] hold to a literal interpretation of the Genesis creation narrative.[90] Though there may be differences in their interpretations, as should be expected between the literalists and allegorists, they nonetheless rejected the

---

86. Clement of Alexandria, *Stromata* 6.16, in *The Ante-Nicene Fathers*, vol. 2.

87. See Thomas G. Weinandy, *Athanasius: A Theological Introduction*, in *Great Theologians* (Burlington, UK.: Ashgate, 2007).

88. Augustine, *The City of God* 12.10, in *The Nicene and Post-Nicene Fathers* Series 1, vol. 2.

89. Ambrose, *Hexaemeron* 1.10.3-7, in Ambrose, *Hexameron, Paradise, and Cain and Abel*, trans. John J. Savage, in *The Fathers of the Church* (Washington, DC.: Catholic Univ. of Amer. Pr., 1961), 42:42-43.

90. See Mook, "The Church Fathers on Genesis, the Flood, and the Age of the Earth," in *Coming to Grips with Genesis*, 23-52.

notion of an old earth, resisting the influence of Greek natural philosophy in this area of thought.

This fact is significant, because progressive creationism certainly is not a *modern* idea (though it is novel in the church), it has in fact been the tendency of ancient civilizations to "impose a theistic meaning upon the almost universal pagan evolutionary philosophies of antiquity."[91] In most cases, the material universe was perceived to be in some way eternal, a belief which sought to discard the need for an omnipotent, holy, eternal, personal, creator God. And thus, what we witness is that, based on early church history, progressive creationists are actually on the wrong side. This is due to the fact that the historical support that they seek are with the ancient *pagan* nations, while biblical creationists find that the teachings of the early church affirm the right and true interpretation of Genesis 1-3, agreeing with the self-witness of Scripture as creation in six days, and only a few thousands of years ago.

91. Morris and Morris, *The Modern Creation Trilogy*, Vol. 1, 75.

CHAPTER

8

CONCLUDING
REMARKS

OUR ANSWER TO THE question of origins then must be in accordance with the testimony of the Word of God, for to posit any alternative interpretations would be to undermine the Christian doctrine of God and the Christian world-and-life view as a whole. It is, after all, creation as per the literal reading of Genesis 1-3 which, according to biblical scholar John Currid:

> provides the context out of which the rest of the biblical narrative, with all its many dimensions, develops. It not only set the Hebrew worldview over against its ancient counterparts but also supplied Western thought with its distinctive account of origins well into the modern period.[92]

Over and against the false interpretations of progressive creationism, theistic evolution, and ancient cosmology (or functionalism), Scripture teaches that God created the world in six days, and only a few thousands of years ago. It is only the interpretation

---

92. Currid, "The Hebrew World-and-Life View," in *Revolutions in Worldview*, 49.

provided by Scripture, and extracted by careful exegesis, that faithfully exhibits and preserves the biblical character and attributes of God as holy, just, omnipotent, omniscient, perfect, truthful, good, sovereign, transcendent, providential, merciful, loving and personal. And which, furthermore, maintains a clear Creator-creation distinction, exclusive to the Christian world-and-life view, which is vital for man's predication (understanding) of reality.

It is only by adopting the same presuppositions of Scripture, viewing and interpreting the world according to the authoritative written revelation of God, that we can make sense of what we see in the world, and that means, also, affirming that what we expect to see is, in fact, what we witness. Whether it be the lunar recession rate,[93] preserved dinosaur hemoglobin,[94]

---

93. See D. DeYoung, "The Earth-Moon System," in eds., R.E. Walsh and C.L. Brooks, *Proceedings of the Second International Conference on Creationism* 2:79-84 (1990).

94. See Mary Schweitzer and T. Staedter, "The Real Jurassic Park," *Earth* (June 1997), 55-57.

the increased salt levels in the sea,[95] earth's magnetic field decay,[96] or any other fact or evidence of God's creation, it is only by thinking God's thoughts after Him, that is to say, presupposing His revealed truth, or allowing His propositional revelation to shape our thinking, that we are able to make sense of such things, all while the natural man ponders to himself in the dark, lost in his intellectual inconsistency and futility. The Christian world-and-life view is the only philosophy of life which provides the preconditions of intelligibility for the predication of reality, or in other words, what must be presupposed in order to make sense of our reality, that being the very same presuppositions of Scripture.

---

95. See S.A. Austin and D.R. Humphreys, "The Sea's Missing Salt: A Dilemma for Evolutionists," in eds., R.E. Walsh and C.L. Brooks, *Proceedings of the Second International Conference on Creationism* 2:79-84 (1990), 17-33.

96. See Sarfati, "The Earth's Magnetic Field: Evidence That the Earth is Young," *Creation* 20(2):15-19 (March-May 1998).

SCRIPTURE INDEX

STEVEN R. MARTINS is a Christian thinker and writer, founding director of the Cántaro Institute and founding pastor of Sevilla Chapel in St. Catharines, ON. He has worked in the fields of missional apologetics and church leadership for ten years and has spoken at numerous conferences, churches, and University student events. He has also contributed articles to *Coalición por el Evangelio* (TGC in Spanish) and the *Siglo XXI* journal of Editorial CLIR. Steven holds a Master's degree *summa cum laude* in Theological Studies with a focus on Christian apologetics from Veritas International University (Santa Ana, CA., USA) and a Bachelor of Human Resource Management from York University (Toronto, ON., Canada). Steven is married to Cindy and they live in Lincoln, Ontario, with their sons Matthias, Timothy, and Nehemías.

www.ingramcontent.com/pod-product-compliance
Lightning Source LLC
Chambersburg PA
CBHW071203120626
46546CB00006B/2395